God At War
The Day God Decided To Flex His Muscles

By Antonio T. Smith, Jr.

Copyright © 2017 by Antonio T. Smith, Jr.

ATS Publishing
2915 Ave M 1/2
Galveston, Texas 77568
www.theatsjr.com/ats-publishing

Ordering Information:
Quantity sales. Special discounts are available on quantity purchases by corporations, associations, and others. For details, contact the publisher at the address above.
Orders by U.S. trade bookstores and wholesalers. Please contact Big Distribution: Tel: (281) 816-7753 or visit www.theatsjr.com/ats-publishing

Printed in the United States of America

Publisher's Cataloging-in-Publication data
Smith, Jr., Antonio T.
God At War : When God decided to flex his muscles / Antonio T. Smith, Jr.
p. cm.
ISBN 978-0-9988207-3-6
Religion & Spirituality

First Edition

Table of Contents

About The Author

Antonio T. Smith, Jr. is an Amazon bestselling author of self-help books. His book Keep Walking received starred reviews from countless journals around the world. Smith graduated from the Houston Baptist University twice. First, with his bachelors of arts in Christianity, as the president of the Theta Kappa Alpha Religious Studies and Theology Honor Society. Second, with his Masters of Arts in Theological Studies, while graduating with the highest GPA in his class. Smith, has served as pastor of a small Baptist church in Galveston, Texas for over five years, and in one of the most sought after preachers in south east Texas. He travels the world giving theological lectures and has taught classes such as Eschatology, Old Testament, New Testament, Paul and His Letters, and Old Testament Covenants, in a few colleges and universities in the Greater Houston Area.

Smith is a prolific public speaker, certified by Les Brown, the world's #1 motivational speaker, who has delivered over 2000 keynotes at events such as the University of Houston, Wiley College, which you can listen to on his podcast. Antonio is an internationally recognized trainer and speaker, and best-selling author in self-help and religious categories. He specializes in Cognitive Behavior Therapy, Business and Strength Training, Leadership, Teleconference Presentations, Personal Breakthroughs, Prosperity Consciousness, Mindset Training, and all levels of effective marketing, as well as scholarship in the Old Testament and Jewish Covenants, and he owns one of the most successful technology companies in

Texas. He holds a bachelor's in Christianity and a Master's in Theological Studies.

Antonio is a best-selling author and a popular podcast host, with a show that reaches 70 countries and 60 different languages.

Antonio T. Smith, Jr. has been coaching people around the world on personal transformation for the last 9 years and reaches over hundreds of thousands of listeners across the globe.

Antonio overcame abandonment, homelessness and brokenness, Antonio had to learn at age six how to use his mind to climb out of sleeping in a dumpster. He would spend his entire childhood homeless, was adopted when he was 14, and aged out of CPS custody at 18 years old. This Galveston, TX native has been through more in his 30+ years than most will ever experience. He has developed a "plant better" attitude, in which he teaches people to plant better seeds in order to have a better life, and has developed coaching tools, programs, courses and books designed to help the world succeed. Today he is a certified Les Brown Partner, a world renown public speaker, and leadership coach.

GOD AT WAR

Introduction

"Depart from here and turn eastward and hide

yourself by the brook Cherith, which is east of the Jordan."[1]

It is with this instruction that the Lord God, who is

YHWH[2], would change not only the narrative of Israel but

would show is power as the one true and living God. Paul

R . House, in his book *Old Testament Theology*, describes

the way YHWH reintroduces himself the world as "The

God Whose Word Shapes History."[3] Indeed House captures

the power and beauty of both first and second Kings

---

[1] 1 Kings 17:3 ESV

[2] YHWH will be used throughout this paper to put the reader's mind into the mindset of the covenants. This is done to drive home how important the lens of the covenants are to understand the significance of the brook Cherith. When YHWH is used, it is used to bring to light the name and emotion that Elijah and others during his time would have felt when thinking or reading of the God as we know today. When the word "God" is used, it is used from a 3rd person narrative point of view to switch the reader back to the 21st century mindset.

[3] *Old Testament Theology*, Paul R. House, p 249.

wonderfully with this description, but how does the Brook Cherith tie into to the complex narrative of God as seen through the Nation of Israel.

When discussing the significance of the Brook Cherith, one must answer one major question and then tackle one major issue: Is there anything significant about the brook Cherith and where is the biblical proof of this significance? When one views the meta-narrative, a grand view common to all of the Old Testament, one would discover that God frequently makes people and places significant throughout His narrative. This significant-making practice of God can be seen from the beginning of time with the Creation Covenant.[4] This covenant plays a

major role in what God will do later in 1 Kings 16 and 18,

which is just before the brook Cherith and immediately

after respectively. The Creation Covenant[5] is the central

theme to the argument of this paper and explaining the

---

[4] The Creation Covenant can be originally read in Genesis 1-2, however the Creation Covenant mentioned here speaks specifically Genesis 6:17-18, which W.J. Dumbrell describes in his book *Covenant and Creation, A Theology of Old Testament Covenants*. The biblical text here reads: "For behold, I will bring a flood of waters upon the earth, to destroy all flesh in which is the breath of life from under heaven; everything that is on earth shall die. But I will establish my covenant with you; and you shall come into the ark, you, your sons, your wife, and your son's wives with you." RSV.

[5] "In this reference we meet for the first time in its some two hundred and ninety occurrences in the Old Testament the Hebrew word berit (ברית), normally translated as 'covenant' in most English versions. The speaker in Genesis 6:17-18 is God, while the person addressed is Noah. What is being said in these two verses reflects immediately upon a decision which has just been taken. God plans virtually to bring to an end all forms of human and animate life in the universe with the account of whose origins the earlier chapters of Genesis have been concerned. A s of divine interventions had resulted in the creation of a world which God had then pronounced as 'very good', e.g., as conforming to the divine intention in every way. The successive episodes in the Book of Genesis which have brought us to the threat of Gen. 6:17-18 have witnessed progressive and increasing attempts by the human race to thwart divine purposes. The result of all this has been the content of these verses which is the divine decision taken and now announced to blot out every living thing from off the earth. Apart from Noah and his immediate family all animate life is to cease." *Covenant and Creation*, W.J. Dumbrell p 11.

significance of the brook Cherith. It is because of the violation of this covenant that provokes God to act in a way in human history that He has never done before, and use a prophet and a location to lead change into the world as well as show His true power as He has never done before. This one argument, which is the violation of the Creation Covenant provokes God into anger, thus resulting God to raise a prophet and not a king and showing His power through the usage of the brook Cherith, will be trifurcated into three simple and smaller arguments: YHWH hates idols, YHWH must make himself seen as the one true God, and the world wants comprise and YHWH refuses to comprise.[6]

---

[6] This argument is an adaptation of the argument presented in *Old Testament Theology*, Paul R. House, p.259, with slight changes.

YHWH HATES IDOLS- SECTION ONE

Background

Back to the beginning of time like a time machine with a destination for creation. God has created the earth and made it perfect and decided to give mankind dominion over what He has created. Man fails to do things God's way, thus ushering in an age of the opposite of what God intended for mankind that has not yet ended. The good news, God has not allowed mankind to endure this opposite reality alone. Viewing the meta-narrative of God through covenantal lenses, one would be able to deduce that there are 5 covenants God has created for man, in order for man to regain his perfection status God had originally intended for them.[7] These covenants are the Creation Covenant,

---

[7] Four of which are currently active or in use during the days of Elijah the prophet and the Brook Cherith, unless you include Deut 30 within the argument as I have.

previously discussed, the Abrahamic Covenant, Mosaic Covenant, Davidic Covenant, and the New Covenant.[8] One could argue that God has revealed each covenant to His people, if one was to include Deuteronomy 30 into the fold, thus proving, that by this day and age, the people were sinning and moving backward from not only the commandments of God but His covenant. Without both sides doing what they have promised to do respectively, there can be no covenant. Obviously, YHWH did not relent on His side of the covenant, but unfortunately His people, both the northern and southern kingdom did, especially the northern kingdom relented. They made a promise to God to follow His commandments and fulfill His covenants, but they did the exact opposite. They turned their back on God and began to worship idols, and YHWH hates idols.

---

[8] The Abrahamic Covenant is found is Gen 12 and 17, Mosiac is found in Exodus 19-20 and Deut 5-6, 27-30, Davidic is found in 2 Samuel 7, Ps 2,8,9,110 and 2Chron 17, and the New Covenant is found in Deut 30:1, Jer 31, Ezekiel 36-37, and Joel 2.

House argues, "With the spread of Baalism as a viable religion in Israel through the support of Ahab and Jezebel (1 Kings 16: 2-33), those who attempt to serve Yahweh must combat a growing public perception that Mosaic faith is no longer viable."[9] In short, Baalism is spreading faster than the Mosiac faith and the Mosiac faith is beginning to be seen as just another religion that can be used as convenient if even used at all.[10] YHWH, being the omniscient God that He is, was fully aware that if He allowed the mixing of Baal and the Mosaic faith to continue, the Mosaic faith would have ceased to exist within a single generation. Therefore, something needed to

---

[9] *Old Testament Theology*, Paul R. House, p 259.

[10] Baal is known as the supreme fatality god on the Canaanites. The Canaanite religion had a strong influence on the Hebrews. During Ahab's reign, however, the name became associated with the worship and rites of the Tryrian deity introduced into Samaria by Jezebel. Temples of Baal at Samaria and Jerusalem are mentioned in 1 Kings 16:21 and 2 Kings 11:18. They had been erected at the time when the Ahab dynasty endeavored to ruse the Yahweh worshipers and the Baal worshipers into a single people under the name national Tryrian god. *The International Standard Bible Encyclopedia*, Geoffrey W. Bromiley (chief editor), pp 377-378.

happen quickly to save the Mosaic faith and it needed to happen by no one other than God.

A Tale of the Opposites

In the region of the Promised Land, the believers of the one true God have become the minority, not the majority. This is eerily similar to the climate found in Genesis 6 and the aforementioned Creation Covenant. God has intervened to give man what He does not deserve, which is His original intention for mankind, but now God must intervene and give man what he actually deserves, mass extermination. However, God has made a promise that he would not destroy the world again through water, and the righteousness of God prevails yet again. YHWH keeps his word when man does not. Man survives mass extinction because God is worthy of keeping His word. So what is God to do? How is He going to correct mankind, and save the remnant that remains? Simple, he does the exact same thing He did before, but in a completely opposite manner. During the Creation covenant, a time before one could call the faith of the one true living God the Mosaic faith, God called for mass extension; however, during the time of the brook Cherith, God mankind live. This pattern continues. Where He used an abundance of water to wipe out mankind, He used a scarcity of water to secure mankind. Where He used four men to repopulate the earth, He used one man to repopulate His religion. Where He would use two kings to unify a kingdom, He would use two prophets to unify the world. The brook Cherith would prove to be much more than just a quick mention in the Old Testament narrative, it would prove to be a dominating show of God and His true power.

King Ahab and Queen Jezebel

It is in this dynamic in which Ahab and Jezebel flourish and spread evil throughout the land. History, both biblical and natural, would have a hard time finding anyone else more responsible that the spread of Baal[11] than Ahab and Jezebel. King Ahab[12] truly lived up to the meaning of his name, "God is a close relative", as he completely defied God and tried to lift Baal to the same superiority as that of YHWH. Jezebel is introduced in the listing of the evils of her husband Ahab's reign.[13] The narrative that includes all three big names in the brook Cherith timeline, Ahab,

[11] The *Oxford Bible Commentary,* edited by John Barton and John Muddiman, writes that Baal is the classic Canannite god of fertility and is responsible for nature's rebirth.

[12] Whose name means the Father is my brother, is the seventh king of Israel and son of Omri. Ahab followed wise a wise policy in defense, entering into alliance with Phoenicia, Judah, and evcen his erstwhile enemies the Arameans. On the other hand, he fell under the influence of his fanatical pagan queen Jezebel, who led him to worship Baal as Yahweh's peer. *The International Standard Bible Encyclopedia, Volume One,* Geoffrey W. Bromiley (chief editor), p. 75.

[13] 1 Kings 16:31.

Jezebel, and Elijah, when combined into one over-arching hidden message, seems to give new meaning to what is really happening behind the scenes of this story and why the brook Cherith becomes so significant. Ahab's "God is a close relative", Jezebel's "Baal is prince",[14] and Elijah's, "Yahweh is my God"[15], all seem to point to a spiritual battle that is more important than any current political agenda or natural drought. While two of the three parties wants to prove that they are either a close relative to God or Baal is a close relative to Him, Elijah seems to have been called by God Himself to prove that there is only one true God and that God is YHWH.

While Ahab and Jezebel have their own agenda by making Baal the national deity and eventually the only or

---

[14] Jezebel's name invokes Baal "the prince". *The International Standard Bible Encyclopedia, Volume Two,* Geoffrey W. Bromiley (chief editor), p 1058.

[15] *Old Testament Theology,* Paul R. House, p.260.

main deity, God has His own agenda by proving that only He is the God of both the spiritual and natural.

The truth in this section is simple and clear. YHWH hates idols and idol worshippers now outnumber YHWH worshippers. Something must be done.

An Abrupt Appearance and the Dominance of God's

Prophets

The world is at the precipice of moral destruction

and eternal damnation. Everyone has heard but no one is

using them to hear the only truth. Baal is now seen as the

God who controls nature and even rebirths it, while YHWH

is seen as irrelevant and common. Mankind lives his life

according to the desires of his heart, and some would say

that evil is winning and more popular than good, or at least

it seems. This is the setting in which the world finds itself,

to include the YHWH's chosen people. Synchronization

has quickly eroded the very fabric of the Mosaic faith and it

is becoming extent, and then appears Elijah. There is no

warning of his appearance, no background information; no

artful transition of the narrative, there is only Elijah.

"Suddenly, with abrupt impetuosity, the mighty figure of Elijah the prophet bursts on the scene like a lightning on the midnight sky. Like Melchizedek, Elijah was without father, mother, or decent. He appears before us unannounced as 'Elijah the Tishbite"[16] and he ushers in a new era of how God tells His story. Another writer pens it this way, "When Ahab, who was not satisfied with the sin of Jeroboam II had introduced the worship of Baal as the national religion in the north, and Jezebel, who was persecuting the prophets of Judah, the prophets who had a direct line to YHWH the one true living God in the south, the Lord raised up the most powerful of all the prophets, namely Elijah the Tishbite."[17] God needed a savior for his people and it proved to be too daunting of a task for a king,

[16] *The Complete Biblical Library, Volume 7 Study Guide.* P. 232.

[17] *Commentary on the Old Testament,* Keil and Delilzsch, p. 161.

and it was too early for His son, thus, He called upon a prophet.

1 Kings 17 chapter would mark not only the power of God manifesting itself in the person of Elijah, but it would also shift the focus of God's narrative from kings to prophets. The kings would no longer dominate the narrative of God, both Hebrew and pagan, but the prophets would. God's word would take precedence in God's plan and his narrative and that word would be distributed by the prophets of God, not the kings of man. From the brook Cherith timeline and forward, God's narrative and the major characters of the Bible would be largely told through the prophets, by the prophets, and to the people. God would establish His dominance throughout Biblical times and He would do the same through the prophets.

One could argue that Elijah is called to restore order in the world, but Thomas C. Oden argues, "But the main reason why Elijah was sent was for Jezebel. Whose pride the Lord wanted to humiliate and whose false hood he wanted to disclose. She had actually appointed herself as minister of Baal and had entrusted herself with the religious service for the god. She also proclaimed that Baal was the supreme god who ruled over those living in heaven and on earth sent rain, watered the skies, and gave fertility to the ground."[18] Obviously, Jezebel promoting Baal as the supreme god would strike fury from YHWH, who has proven to be a jealous God. There is no one more supreme than YHWH and YHWH had spent centuries proving His power in miraculous ways. He created the world by simply speaking it into existence. He created man from the ground. He sent ten plagues that affected the Egyptians but left the Hebrew nation untouched. He parted the Red Sea, He cared for the Children of the Wilderness for forty years. YHWH

---

[18] *Ancient Christian Commentary on Scripture,* Thomas C Oden, p. 99.

had done so many different things to prove His power and supremacy and now within two generations His faith was becoming obsolete and was currently being threatened by a pagan queen named Jezebel.

The promotion of Baal as the only god of those living in heaven was sure to provoke YHWH's anger when it is God who created both the Heaven and the Earth. To say that Baal is the god of the holy place that YHWH had created for His self to reside would most certainly lead to provoking His anger. Then there is the watering of the skies and sending rain. Returning to the central theme, which is the Creation Covenants, the significance of the brook Cherith, and how God is at war, YHWH created the world and also has the power to destroy it. It is He who calls out to the water and it obeys His voice. It is He who caused the mountains to rise from the ground and to touch the skies. Therefore, it is certainly He who can control when it does and does not rain. God is the God of nature and Baal is not. This becomes the sign, or significance, of the brook Cherith. When Ahab and Jezebel are promoting that their god controls nature and even the spiritual, God uses the brook to show how He and He alone controls nature.

"The policies and actions of Ahab and Jezebel are intended to promote Baal as the national deity of Israel in place of Yahweh."[19] Baal wasn't just being promoted, but he was being used to replace God. How can the Creator be replaced? Had YHWH allowed for Himself to be replaced or even diluted by Baal, then there would be no Christianity today. If YHWH claimed to be the one true God, but allowed another god to thwart Him out of His position, then there would be no hope in the resurrection that was to come. The hope for the future hope would be lost and there would be absolutely no reason to believe in a single

---

[19] *IVP Bible Background Commentary Old Testament,* John H. Walton, Victor H. Matthews, Mark W. Chavalas. p. 376.

covenant that YHWH had given. If the one true God could be overthrown by any other god, or a king or a queen, then the one true God would not be God at all. He would simply cease to exist or just become another god amongst so many.

If there was ever a time for YHWH to reestablish His existence and prominence amongst man and other gods, this would be it. Certainly, YHWH did not need to prove Himself to anyone, He could have simply exterminated mankind through other means than water and started over from the beginning, but God's righteousness can only be outweighed by His steadfast love. It was His love that allowed YHWH to prove His existence and dominance because if He would have decided to give the world His righteousness, He could have simply proved His existence and supremacy by destroying everything that lived. What the world deserved at the time was for YHWH to show his existence in their deaths. Then they would have seen who the one true God was.

House brings to light an interesting fact. Two men, Elijah and Elisha, serve as the chief preachers and theologians who press the Yahwists' claims, and they are joined by other named and unnamed prophets who suffer for covenantal fidelity. For the first time, the canon links prophetic proclamation and suffering, a combination that will endure through the rest of the Old Testament. Commitment to the truth may be the right lifestyle to uphold, but it is not a safe lifestyle to choose.[20] As said before, YHWH's champions of His message would shift from kings to preachers and this would start a trend that would continue into the New Testament and into the modern day earth. Although YHWH's message is compelling and rewarding, the carrier of His message is

---

[20] *Old Testament Theology,* Paul R. House, p. 260.

often brutally attacked, as well as frequently, and trouble seems to follow the one who carries YHWH's message. In many cases, the one who has been called to carry the message of God will be burned with the pain of His enemies. In this case, Elijah suffers from this inevitable fate of the prophet.

God as the God of Nature

Regardless of how much Elijah suffers at the hands of his enemies, he still pushes forth God's message. He begins by proving that YHWH is the God of nature and not Baal. "Elijah's career strikes at the very tenets of syncretism and Baalism. His name means "Yahweh is my God," and he believes it his mission to help others make this confession instead of declaring allegiance to Baal. He promises there will be no rain until he says so[21] because Baalists believed their god made rain, unless, of course, it

---

[21] 1 Kings 17:1

was dry season and he needed to be raised from the dead.[22]
YHWH was not viewed as the deity who controlled the
rain, instead, it was Baal who was widely accepted as the
god of nature. However, Elijah would walk to the king and
tell him that his God, the God of Abraham, Isaac, and
Jacob, would close the heavens and there would be no more
rain to come. With one statement Elijah was proving two
things: Baal was not the god of nature but YHWH was and
Baal was a local god and YHWH was not.

Elijah also pushes for a commitment to just one
god, not both. He urged the people to either serve Baal or
YHWH and later in the showdown at Mt Carmel, Elijah
would prove that there is only one true God and this God
can do what Baal cannot. The brook Cherith will soon
prove that God rules over nature in a way that eliminates
the nature god Baal from consideration as a living deity.

------

[22] *Old Testament Theology*, Paul R. House, p. 260.

The Introduction and Significance of the Brook Cherith

Elijah sent a clear message to the King Ahab and Queen Jezebel. He defied their power by giving them bad news, he defied their god by telling them that his God will close the skies, and he did both boldly and stood flat-footed in the power of those who had a more physical authority and power than he did. As a result, Elijah needed shelter from the queen. She wanted his head and Elijah feared her wrath and had good reason to do so. "Elijah needed shelter from the king and the queen. He also needed shelter and provision because of the drought which would last over three years. His water supply would be the brook Cherith and his food supply would be, perhaps the most selfish of all birds."[23] First, there is the issue of the shelter from the king and queen. Elijah, a man of YHWH is in fear of his life and must now flee in order to keep it. Baal is against

---

[23] *The Complete Biblical Library, Volume 7 Study Guide.*

him because Elijah has claimed the YHWH will close the skies when that is *only* a job that Baal himself can accomplish. There is also a need for shelter because the king and the queen have great power and authority and have made alliances with neighboring kingdoms. Therefore, there is nowhere Elijah can go where the royalty of Ahab and Jezebel cannot reach, as well as the power of Baal, as he is the god of nature. Elijah is in a bad place with an angry god and some bad people. Yet, YHWH is still able. He instructs Elijah to "get thee hence, and turn thee eastward, and hide thyself by the brook Cherith."[24] YHWH would instruct Elijah to drink from the brook and I have commanded the ravens to feed thee there.[25] This demanded great faith because the brook that ran through the Kidron was a wadi, a stream that flowed only during the rainy

---

[24] 1 Kings 17:3 KJV

[25] 1 Kings 17:4 KJV

season.[26] Moments before Elijah was told by YHWH to tell the king that there will be no rain or dew for years to come, Elijah is told travel to a water source that is will surely be dried up, along with everything else that depends on rain to survive or be its source of life. This is a leap of faith that Elijah must take, but YHWH will use this leap of faith to prove how powerful He is. This brook was hardly a long term solution to the drought that Elijah initiated with the power of YHWH. In addition, YHWH has declared that ravens will feed Elijah. To a twenty-first century Christian, this sounds normal or less impressive, but ravens are scavengers, not providers. Ravens? Have people ever been fed by ravens? Certainly not, ravens are untrained beasts of nature and no god can control what a raven does, until the brook Cherith and the YHWH God. The brook Cherith becomes significant in the narrative of God because

---

[26] *Holman Old Testament Commentary,* Gary Inrig.

YHWH uses it to show His dominion over nature and the lack of Baal's. Several scriptures teach that God provides food even for the ravens and their young,[27] but here, instead of God feeding the ravens, the ravens are now feeding God's servant.[28] Ravens are wild animals, yet at the brook YHWH keeps them tamed. Ravens are scavengers but at the brook, YHWH makes them providers. Ravens are fed by YHWH, but at the brook, God uses them to feed his servant. Baal could do none of these things, but he was proclaimed to be the god of nature. Additionally, the brook Cherith was in the territory of Baal, yet Baal had no power to stop YHWH from providing water and life to His servant.

The brook, continues to show YHWH's power because it should have dried up in the drought, but it lasts

---

[27] Job 38:41, Psalm 147:9, Luke 12:24

[28] *Cornerstone Biblical Commentary,* William H. Barnes. p. 149.

until He provides for a widow for another blessing. And the ravens, the ravens are considered unclean birds,[29] yet Elijah is fed by the ravens and then later fed by the Sidonian woman. These are two things that God has deemed unclean: one an animal and the other a pagan, which in the eyes of some Hebrew people is an animal. Yet YHWH uses all three to bless his servant. First, the brook gives life to Elijah, as water is the life source of all living things. In a world slowly dying from lack of water, as well as the lack of YHWH in their lives, life is restored to Elijah via a brook that should have run dry. This proves to the readers of 1 Kings that God is the God of nature because He can make all things in nature obey Him, including a brook that has no consciousness or will. If one were to look through the lens of the covenants, one could deduce that in the beginning water obeyed YHWH, at the brook water obeyed

---

[29] Leviticus 11:5, Deuteronomy 14:14

YHWH, and when Jesus spoke rebuked the in the Book of Mark, watered obeyed YHWH again, this time He was wrapped in flesh and told us to call Him Jesus. God has definitely proved that He is more "god of nature" than Baal is. Baal is no god at all. God is the one true and living God.

Later in the chapter, YHWH would use a pagan widow to bless Elijah and to feed him and care for his needs, all within Baal territory. YHWH purposely defies the power of Baal in his own territory to prove that He is the one true and living God.

YHWH proves His power by proving that He is not the strongest God, but the only God. The brook Cherith proves that YHWH is not just the local deity, but it also proves that YHWH can do things that Baal cannot. The challenge at Mt. Carmel[30] proves that YHWH hears

---

[30] 1 Kings 18: 16-40.

prophets while Baal has no ability to do so.[31] Baal has no

voice to speak to his prophets or an ear to hear their pleas.

Once again proving that YHWH can do things that Baal

can never do, and also prove that Baal is not real.

"Already the drought had laid on the land some six

months,[32] now the reason for it all was to reveal to Israel's

apostate leadership that the message was clear. Israel had

broken the pledge of its covenantal relationship with God.[33]

This was God demonstrating His concern for both his

people's infidelity, and for trusting in fertility gods like

Baal."[34] The covenants had already been established and

Israel had promised to follow and obey them. They would

do their end of the deal while YHWH upheld His. For their

---

[31] *Old Testament Theology*. Paul R. House. p. 260.

[32] Luke 4:25; James 5:17; 1 Kings 18:1

[33] Deuteronomy 11:16-17, 28:23-24; Leviticus 26:19; 1 Kings 8:35

[34] *The Expositor's Bible Commentary*, Gaebelien, p. 138

obedience, they would receive life, land, and descendants. However, in lieu of their sinful ways and their worshipping of other idols, they would receive the exact opposite. Where there was once life, the people would now receive death. Where there was land, they would now receive exile, and where there were descendants they would enmity. The covenants were violated, especially the creation covenant and Israel deserved mass extinction but instead, they would get the brook, a drought, and a display of YHWH's power.

More Significance and the Paralleling of Elijah to Moses

The brook Cherith is somewhere east of the Jordan, which marked the eastern border of the land given to Israel. On a purely physical level, it functions (unlike the Jordan) as a place far away and hidden from King Ahab who was seeking Elijah's life because of the drought. The name Cherith means a "cutting" or "separation." This becomes significant both physically and spiritually. Elijah was cut off from the world physically, as God hid him from the reach of Ahab's arms. Simultaneously, the Cherith represents a spiritual "cutting off". Elijah was completely cut off from all things, but the power and grace of God. God would cut Elijah off in order to grow him spiritually. In truth, Elijah's ministry would have been a successful one, as he stood up to an evil king and prophesied a drought to come that surely did. By all accounts, his ministry was a success and he was willing to be used by God. However, God was not through with Elijah yet. There was a greater task to be accomplished in the next chapter, but God had to use the better part of three years to prepare Elijah to be totally dependent upon Him for the daunting task that was to come. It is at the brook, Elijah would discover that to be cut off with God is actually to be multiplied by God.

The language of "cutting off" is continued in the next chapter.[35] While Jezebel is "cutting off" the prophets in the land, Ahab has Obadiah to try to find pasture to save the animals from having to be "cut off." Ravens were known to not even feed their own young[36] so it is a serious indictment on Ahab and Jezebel— two people who cared more about the lives of animals than the lives of the prophets, while God would make sure unclean ravens— animals who neglect their own young, cared more for God's prophet. This indictment against the ravens is shifted from the unclean ravens, in the second half of the chapter, to the unclean gentiles that Elijah will be charged to protect and bless.

Elijah, however, does not remain "cut off." Just as after the widow's son is revived after Elijah stretches out on

---

35 1 Kings 18: 4-5.

36 Job 38:41; Psalm 147:49

him three times, so after three years, Elijah returns from the brook to confront Ahab and defeat Baal. All of this is a mockery of Baal, who as the storm god was supposed to bring rain on the earth. Of course, the drought is a direct assault on the claims of Baal, but so is the death and resurrection theme. It is explained that the reason Baal did not always bring rain on the earth was that Mot, the god of death, would kill him every year and then his sister Anat would eventually take revenge on Mot and free Baal from death.[37] Instead, it is shown that Yahweh is the one who has control over rain and life and death.

Beyond being a symbol of death, the brook is also a symbol of the wilderness. The author of Kings draws a number of parallels throughout the book between Elijah and Moses who was before him. Both appear before a

---

[37] *The International Standard Bible Encyclopedia, Volume One,* p. 121.

wicked ruler. Both flee for their lives. Both fast for forty days and forty nights. Both experience wind, earthquake, and fire up on a mountain. Both prepare an altar consumed by God's fire from heaven. The parallel of Elijah to Moses is strikingly clear and intentional. YHWH used Moses to deliver His people from physical bondage, now YHWH uses Elijah to deliver His people from spiritual bondage.

Similarly here, the notion of drinking from the brook and being miraculously fed with bread and meat while in the land east of the Jordan reminds the intended reading audience of the author of Kings of Moses and Israel in the wilderness being fed with bread and quail from heaven. This is why it is not the Jordan itself that Elijah drinks from; rather he is east of the Jordan, outside of the land, in order to show that Elijah is a new Moses and Ahab a new Pharaoh. The brook Cherith is the sign of a new beginning by the same YHWH.

YHWH REFUSES TO COMPROMISE – SECTION THREE

Blatant Vessels of YHWH

When YHWH needed to make a stance of great power to prove that He is the God of nature, He didn't use mighty rushing waves of water, He used a peaceful stream that should not have lasted close to three years without a renewing source of rain. When He could have shown His might with a great force of waves, He showed His power with a peaceful brook in the territory of Baal. Only God can do such a thing with such grace and power. When the YHWH faith was under attack by a militarily great king and queen, YHWH did not raise up an army to defeat this evil, rather, He used two men who were armed with the word of the Lord, Elijah, and Elisha.[38] Two men would eventually defeat an army of evil because YHWH's

---

[38] *Holman Old Testament Commentary*, Gary Inrig, p. 133.

strength is not in numbers, but in His Self. Both Elijah and the brook become blatant tools for God to use to show his might. In one case, a man closes the sky, defeats an army of prophets and proves that YHWH is the one and true living God. In the other case, a small section of water is used to save the life of God's servant while wild and tame fewer ravens feed Elijah with great obedience. Elijah's name means YHWH is my God, while the brook lies in Baal territory and blesses Elijah while Baal can do absolutely nothing about it. All these things, the brook, the ravens, and the prophet are used to become blatant tools to prove that YHWH is the God of nature and everything.

Yahwehists are either outnumbered or outspoken, either way, the world wants to compromise their beliefs and YHWH does not like compromise. Syncretism is the law of the land and most people are taking what they like from one god and then taking what they like from another god until they have arrived at the God that better serves their needs. They are not allowing YHWH to make them in His image; instead, they want YHWH to be made in their image, while many temples are to be resurrected throughout to land to make worship comfortable for the people. The travel is too far. Those who live in the northern kingdom should not have to journey to Jerusalem three times or more a year. Therefore, compromises are made and only YHWH suffers. The merging of two gods, Baal and YHWH is preferred but the author of the Creation Covenant refuses to blend in with any other god, thus he uses the brook, the prophet, and the ravens to stand out.

It is clear that YHWH intends to prove that Baal is out of contention for consideration for a living deity. In the midst of the drought, YHWH demonstrated that He, not Baal was the God of nature who could provide all the resources that Elijah would ever require.[39] This would prove to be crucial training for the later event at the Mt Carmel. At the brook, Elijah would learn how to have faith and depend on YHWH with absolute reliability. The brook would prove to be a symbol of God's power and a resource to teach Elijah on the total dependency of his YHWH. The Brook Cherith Narrative would serve God in all His purposes centuries after it had dried up.

The ravens play a key role in proving the significance of the brook Cherith when one is to think about what actually happened. It has already been discussed that the ravens were wild scavengers that were not providers, but YHWH made them otherwise. However, there is something more notable than the ravens feeding Elijah by mouth; it is what they fed him that is more impressive: bread and meat. These are generous provisions;

---

[39] *Holman Old Testament Commentary*, Gary Ingrid, pp. 133-134.

rarely would meat be eaten by common people during the days of the brook Cherith, but it was even rarer that they would eat meat twice a day.[40] It is quite likely that until Elijah went to the brook, he had never eaten meat twice a day in his entire life. Yet, in a drought when animals were surely scarce and dying, YHWH manages to feed Elijah meat twice daily. This is incredible and unusual. YHWH proves that He is the God of nature and also that He is a God that does more than what anyone deserves.

[40] *Cornerstone Biblical Commentary,* Willam H. Barnes, p. 149

Conclusion

To the functionally minded, Elijah's prolonged stay by the brook Cherith looks like a waste of a promising life. Here was the nation's foremost prophet, existing in isolation in the middle of nowhere. What chance had he now of addressing the king and court, or of leading a spiritual revival? But God's ways truly are not ours, not even close. The time had not yet come to send him back to lock tusks again with Ahab and Jezebel, who definitely wanted a piece of the prophet. The time was not yet and God still had more disproving Baal as the god of nature to accomplish.

By leading His servant away from the familiar mountains of Gilead, and from the challenge of exercising a prophetic ministry in a hostile setting, God was offering Elijah not only an extended period of rest from his labor, but a precious opportunity to deepen his closeness to Himself. The stresses Elijah faced here would be of a totally different kind. It would be a stress that leads to a total dependency on God.

Most of us depend on our relationships far more than we realize to grow spiritually. Yet, here was Elijah, a leader, with no one to lead, and a preacher who had no one to preach, but that is how God wanted it. In order for Elijah to effectively become his best for God, he had to first learn how to completely trust in God. That is where the brook plays its part. No one knows the total plan of God, one can only look from a far and deduce what God has already done and gather in one's mind what He is able to do next.

The brook itself is significant because it balances the world. It allows God to re-establish who He is and what He has dominion over. This narrative of the Bible is about more than what God can do after a brook has been dried, it is more about what God has already done and how His people have forgotten His love and His ways, so God begins a new Exodus. When one looks through the lens of the covenants, especially the Creation Covenant and the Mosaic Covenant, one would see that God was simply sticking to his end of the deal. When the unrighteousness of the people excelled, the righteousness of God prevailed. This time, the bondage was not Egyptian chains, but Hebraic sin. However, God had a plan, a prophet, some ravens, and the brook that would change the world and shift the power from kings to prophets that would eventually lay the foundation for Jesus the Christ to over throw all kings. This is the significance of the brook Cherith.

To the functional mind, Elijah prolonged his stay between the brook and his breakthrough. With respect to this method of thinking, there is not much to disagree with. While it is true that Elijah stayed until the brook was depleted of resources, it is also true that Elijah recognized when the Lord depletes one area of your life of resources,

Elijah had enough faith to trust the Lord to provide in the next area of his life. While I have attributed the true meaning of the significance of the brook, this secondary meaning must also be considered. Elijah had the knowledge in who God was to move to the brook, which was not meant to sustain life in the midst of a drought, while simultaneously having the knowledge of the fear Jezebel placed within his own heart. What a detrimental place to find one's self, between one's faith and one's pain.

It is worth mentioning that God slowed Elijah's life down to His speed. Elijah was moving far too swiftly in his own fear. God slowed Elijah to His own faith. The Holy scriptures do not give us insight into the things God may have mentioned to Elijah during this time of crisis, nor do they point to God saying anything at all. Moreover, Elijah spent many days alone. In fact, Elijah spent at least one thousand days alone, according to scriptures. For one thousand days or more, Elijah was slowed to God's pace. I believe this would work well for any of us in today's society. We are moving quickly and have passed up the power of God. Of course, God's power can meet us on our fast-paced journey's, but sometimes God wants us to slow down and allow Him to provide for us. Where there is God there will always be provisions. On the other end of the spectrum, it is quite possible God said nothing to Elijah. All those days and not a word from the Lord. We can imagine that, as months succeeded uneventful months, Elijah became more practiced at seeking the Lord. What a powerful journey Elijah must have traveled— slowly.

Ironically, what does the brook Cherith say to us about God's methods of communication? Surely, there should be no argument among brothers and sisters of the faith that God himself would be the greatest communicator of all time. Yet, we still must wrestle with His silence. One must wonder what does God communicate to us during his periods of silence, some in which can last over a thousand days. In truth, this pericope forces me to wonder does God communicate to us when He is silent, or does He await for us to communicate with Him during His silence. On the one hand, I completely trust that God will never leave us or forsake us, yet the brook gives of evidence, at least textually, that our Lord does not always talk when we want Him to do so. Strangely enough, His silence is insignificant to us when we are waiting on Him for a few days, but it is tormenting to us when we are waiting for His communication for a few years. On the other hand, this pericope proves that God never left Elijah. He didn't have to say a word, his ravens spoke on His behalf— so did the brook. I must admit, I have missed God talking to me throughout my life because I was waiting for words and not looking at my brook.

It is worth mentioning that God proved Himself to Elijah just as much as He proved Himself to King Ahab and Queen Jezebel. God proved to Elijah that He could guide him when no one else could. Elijah's time by the brook was surely designed to maintain his inner life with God and to further prepare him for the ministry that would follow. It should be noted that Elijah was a great prophet, known as "the prophet" and before God used him to complete his ministry God Himself sent Elijah to the wilderness, just as He did our Lord and Savior Jesus Christ. Which leads me to properly understand that whenever our God calls us into to ministry, seclusion is a major movement within our call. Without seclusion, Elijah would not have known the sustaining power of God, nor would he understand the pace of God either. God has His own pace and His own methods, which usually do not match ours. After all, His ways are not our ways and His thoughts are not our thoughts.[41] There

is no doubt that God secludes His anointed. Without

seclusion, one cannot be included in the ministry of God.

This pericope also teaches me how to deal with

being disappointed with God. Throughout my many years

as a minister for God, and even more years as a Christian in

his flock of sheep, I know one thing for sure: Christians are

too "holy" to admit that we grow disappointed in God. If

we are honest with ourselves, we often find a way to have

faith in God and be disappointed in the direction He has for

our lives at the same time. This is very possible, very

accurate, and something I have done many times in my life.

"Dear God, I love you very much, but I am sick and tired of

you not giving me what I want for my life." I cannot

honestly express how many times I have truly felt this way.

---

[41] Isaiah 55:8-9 "For My thoughts are not your thoughts, neither are your ways My ways," declares the LORD. "For as the heavens are higher than the earth, so are My ways higher than your ways, and My thoughts than your thoughts."

Unfortunately, I am being honest. I have suffered from having faith and being disappointed in the One in whom I place my faith. However, I have spent many precious moments of my life disappointed with His actions for it.

I can only imagine how Elijah would have felt. Surely he had great faith in God, all the sacred scriptures prove that, but any person would have been disappointed with being alone for years by a brook, because of their faith. That had to be tormenting, but Elijah handled it epically. Which teaches me everything I will ever need to know about having faith in God but being disappointed in him too. Elijah did two things I most certainly need to master as soon as possible: 1) He stayed when God ordered him to stay, 2) He moved when God dried up the brook. Lord knows I need to work on both of these areas, but don't we all? Elijah stayed when things grew silent. I think we all have the power to stay in our call when times grow rough, but it's much harder to do so when times grow silent. There is something about God's silence and just silence in itself that hurts us. Most of us cannot sit in our own bedrooms without the television or radio filling the room with noise because we can't stand the thought of dealing with ourselves. Silence is a killer of those who are afraid to deal with themselves. Silence hurts me as well. Be that as it may, Elijah conquered his silence because he "stayed". There is the power of Elijah that needs to become the power of Antonio. The power of "stay". Stay does not mean to quit. It doesn't mean to find an excuse to leave or be comfortable, it means to persist well after my comfort has left. This story of Elijah has taught me the staying power of faith. Without it, it is quite difficult to have faith.

Meanwhile, there is the second lesson I was taught during the moments of Elijah's brook Cherith experience. The courage to "move". Elijah moved when his season was over. May the Lord bless all who are able to move in him when we are called to do so. There have been many moments in which I did not move and have paid for it dearly. Staying is one part of the battle, but knowing when to move is the other part. Elijah had the faith to move when others did not. When he moved, God, blessed him abundantly for moving. We should all be so wise and trust God in the same manner of Elijah. Stay and Move. These are the two lessons I will take from this episode of Elijah's ministry. The art of Stay and Move will bless me for years to come.

Ultimately, God will always reveal the reasons for His divine permissions in our lives—His dried-up brooks. We simply have to have the faith to stay in His will and the courage to move when His will takes us down a path that we do not think is best for us. When you place the brook and the ravens into modern life, you arrive at three essential conclusions: Elijah lost his food, water, and shelter. Or, said in another manner, Elijah lost all his money and his provisions. Yet, when it came time for him to trust in God, he trusted. Elijah trusted when he lost everything that was taking care of him. We should all be more like Elijah. I should be more like him. God eventually provided for Elijah through a widow. Which does not make much sense? Yet, God frequently moves in manners that do not make much sense. If Elijah didn't trust in God, He would have never found provisions in the brook. Likewise, if he didn't trust in God, he would not have found a provision in the widow.

In one story, God uses water, which should not have been in existence, ravens that are selfish scavengers, and a gentile widow who has no source of income, to provide for Elijah. God is truly the God of all things. As I leave this passage I am lifted in my vision to see the glory of the God

I am called to trust. I am able to see His absolute sovereignty and power that even birds contrary to natural instincts do His bidding on behalf of His people. I am able to see His unsearchable wisdom in that if humans delivered food they may have divulged the hiding place, if dogs, morning and night, someone might have seen this curiosity and followed. Yet birds carrying food would have aroused no interest. I am able to see His unmatchable grace. Though, He withdraws His Word from a people for a season, He protects that Word, and its servants, for future ministry. God became all things for Elijah. Specifically, concerning this text, God became the source, sovereign, the one who control nature, the method of divine deliverance, the miraculous giving agent, the brook that kept running well after science did its job to end such an event from happening, the ravens that became servants to God's man, the regularity in an irregular situation, the morning and the evening— without fail, the variety of grace, the bread and the meat, and the sufficiency in the midst of insufficiency.

God is still the same! He can still employ anything or anyone to meet the needs of His people, and He will never fail those whose trust is in Him, those who are there.

God has used this pericope to show me that He is the leader moving us forward when our doubt wants us to remain frozen in place. It is clear from the brook Cherith that God has us on a program and if we follow His program, we will be blessed for doing so. We should all be able to trust God and believe in what He can do for us and what He has done for us. We are His creation and we live inside of His creation. Therefore, there is nothing that He cannot do, it is up to us to simply remember this when things become more difficult than we choose to handle.

He wants us to TRUST Him. This is why He allows the brooks to dry up – so that we shall find our all in HIM and lean not on His gifts and provision, but on Himself.

Elijah was like you and I. There was nothing special about him. He was not immune to pain or poverty, in fact, He spent all his life in poverty and in Pain. Yet, he presented himself courageous unto the Lord. He lived during very wicked times. He lived during a succession of seven wicked kings had reigned over Israel: (1) Jeroboam (1 Kings 12:28-33); (2) Nadab (15:25-26); (3) Baasha (15:27-28); (4) Elah, a drunkard and a murderer (16:8-9); (5) Zimri, guilty of treason (16:20); (6) Omri (16:25-26); and (7) Ahab (16:28-33), with whom must be linked his notoriously wicked wife Jezebel. Worship of the true God had all but ceased; Baal-worship had become the national religion, only 7000 Israelites remained true in heart to the Lord, and these were fearful and had hidden their testimony

(1 Kings 19:18). Yet, Elijah preserved. He was relentless, even while he was hiding in fear. He was a man amongst men. God's promise was certain, but Elijah lived during a time filled with uncertainty. Yet, God continued to be faithful, as well as Elijah.

This is a wonderful story about how one can be both full of faith and full of fear, but choose faith to overcome that fear. When God provides what we believe to be meager resources, we should be grateful. What do you do when your brook dries up? When this happens to us sometimes we cry out, "Lord what happened" Where did I go wrong? Didn't you tell me to come here and wait and you would provide for me? How can I be in the center of your will and my brook is drying up?" The reason we think that is because we tend to think that we are in the center of God's will as long as everything is going great. Have you ever considered that you may just be in the center of His will when the brook dries up? When our brook dries up we are tempted to think that God's power has ceased. But drying brooks are not an indication of God forsaking us it is only an indication that God is changing the source of his supply. F.B. Meyer assures us that God knew exactly what he was doing for "God's servants are often called to sit by drying brooks. Many of us have had to sit by drying brooks; perhaps some are sitting by them now – the drying brook of popularity, ebbing away as it did from John the Baptist. The drying brook of health, sinking under a creeping paralysis, or a slow decline. The drying brook of money, slowly dwindling before the demands of sickness, bad debts or other people's extravagance. The drying brook of friendship, which for long has been diminishing, and threatens soon to cease. Ah, it is hard to sit beside a drying brook…. Why does God let them dry? He wants to teach us not to trust in his gifts but in Himself. Let us learn these lessons, and turn from our failing Cheriths to our unfailing

Savior. All sufficiency resides in Him!"[42]

[42] F.B. Meyer. Great Men of the Bible. (London, England; Marshall
Pickering, 1990). pp. 345-346

Bibliography

Barnes, William Hamilton, and Philip Wesley Comfort. *1-2 Kings*. Carol Stream, Ill.: Tyndale House Pub., 2012.

Barton, John. *The Oxford Bible Commentary*. Oxford: Oxford University Press, 2001.

Bromiley, Geoffrey William. *The International Standard Bible Encyclopedia, Volume Three: K-P*. Fully Rev. ed. Grand Rapids, Mich.: W.B. Eerdmans, 1979.

Bromiley, Geoffrey William. *The International Standard Bible Encyclopedia*. Fully Rev. ed. Grand Rapids, Mich.: W.B. Eerdmans, 1979.

Bromiley, Geoffrey William. *The International Standard Bible Encyclopedia, Volume Two: E-J*. Fully Rev. ed. Grand Rapids, Mich.: W.B. Eerdmans, 1979.

Conti, Marco. *1-2 Kings, 1-2 Chronicles, Ezra, Nehemiah, Esther*. Downers Grove, Ill.: InterVarsity Press, 2008.

Cook, F. C. *The Bible Commentary*. Grand Rapids: Baker Book House, 1981.

Dumbrell, William J. *Covenant and Creation: A Theology of Old Testament Covenants*. Eugene, Or.: Wipf & Stock, 2009.

Farrar, F. W. *The Old Testament Study Bible: 1 & 2 Kings*. Springfield, Mo.: World Library Press, 1997.

Gaebelein, Frank E. *The Expositor's Bible Commentary: With the New International Version of the Holy Bible, 1 & 2 Kings, 1 & 2 Chronicles, Ezra, Nehemiah, Esther, Job*. Grand Rapids: Zondervan Pub. House, 1988.

House, Paul R. *Old Testament Theology*. Downers Grove, Ill.: InterVarsity Press, 1998.

Inrig, Gary, and Max E. Anders. *I & II Kings*. Nashville, Tenn.: Broadman & Holman, 2003.

Keil, Carl Friedrich, and Franz Delitzsch. *Commentary on the Old Testament*. Peabody, Mass.: Hendrickson, 1996.

Ripken, Nik, and Gregg Lewis. *The Insanity of God: A True Story of Faith Resurrected*. Nashville, Tenn.: B&H Publishing Group, 2013.

Seow, C. L. *The New Interpreter's Bible*. Nashville, Tenn.: Abingdon, 1999.

Walton, John H., and Victor Harold Matthews. *The IVP Bible Background Commentary: Old Testament*.

www.ingramcontent.com/pod-product-compliance
Lightning Source LLC
Chambersburg PA
CBHW060717030426
42337CB00017B/2905